I've Never Met
an Idiot on the River

Also by Henry Winkler, with Lin Oliver

The Hank Zipzer: The World's Greatest Underachiever series

I've Never Met an Idiot on the River

Reflections on Family, Photography, and Fly-fishing

by
HENRY WINKLER

Introduction by Stacey Winkler

INSIGHT 👁 EDITIONS

San Rafael, California

ISBN: 978-1-60887-020-2

 ROOTS of PEACE   ⚙ REPLANTED PAPER

Insight Editions, in association with Roots of Peace, will plant two trees for each tree used in the manufacturing of this book. Roots of Peace is an internationally renowned humanitarian organization dedicated to eradicating land mines worldwide and converting war-torn lands into productive farms and wildlife habitats. Together, we will plant two million fruit and nut trees in Afghanistan and provide farmers there with the skills and support necessary for sustainable land use.

Manufactured in India

10 9 8 7 6 5 4 3 2 1

INSIGHT 👁 EDITIONS

10 Paul Drive
San Rafael, CA 94903
www.insighteditions.com

To Skip Brittenham and in memory of Leonard Hanzer, for introducing me to a life's passion.

And, always, to Stacey.

"You are about to enter a lifelong journey into a different world."

—Michael D. Shook, *The Complete Idiot's Guide to Fly Fishing*

"If you will it, it is not a dream."

—Theodor Herzl, *Old New Land*

Table of Contents

IT'S NINE O' CLOCK IN THE MORNING IN WEST YELLOWSTONE, MONTANA, AND WE ARE ABOUT TO START OUR DAY ON THE RIVER. HEAVEN ON EARTH.

Ladies First
Stacey Winkler's Side of the Fish Story

When I began dating Henry in the 1970s, I was struck, as most people were, by how incredibly kind and good-natured he was. Henry was such a gentleman and so caring and thoughtful. After a few months of his chivalrous treatment, I kept waiting for his darker side to show up. I'd probably still be waiting for a glimpse of it more than thirty years later, if I had not started fly-fishing with my husband.

Honestly, I've never seen Henry wake up with anything but a smile and an enthusiastic "GOOD MORNING! HOW ARE YOU?" I hear this from him each and every day, and I have no problem telling you that the man I married is still the most thoughtful, kind, and optimistic person I've ever known. Henry's glass is *always* half full, and he is always patient and easygoing—except when he is fly-fishing.

It's odd because Henry is a native New Yorker and we live in Los Angeles. In both of those high-stress places, he is never flustered or overwrought. Only in the serene beauty of fly-fishing country does the crazed and competitive Henry appear.

Now I don't want to give you the impression that he is on edge the whole time we're in the wilderness. Henry's feisty alter ego arises only if someone threatens to cut short his time on the water.

One year in Montana, my calm and loving husband, who has always been shockingly patient with our children, actually threw a wader boot across the room because our daughter, Zoe, then a teenager, was taking too long to prepare for an afternoon of fishing. It didn't help that Henry had given up his morning on the river to join us for a horseback ride. With half the day gone, he was really eager to get in as much fishing as possible before sunset.

Still, I'd never seen him lose his cool like that. It was as if he had turned into Damien, the evil child in *The Omen*. After the boot-hurling incident, we told the children that positioning themselves between their father and the trout was courting disaster. If you happen to find yourself on the same river as Henry, my advice to you is this: Do not obstruct his casting, because he truly believes all fish wear tags reading "To Be Caught and Released Only by Henry Winkler."

MY WIFE IS ONE GREAT-LOOKING FISHER-PERSON!

It's hard to describe just how much Henry looks forward to his Montana trips. With his television roles, scores of speaking engagements, constant travel, production meetings, and all his other responsibilities, Henry is a busy, busy man. He loves acting, writing children's novels, and producing. He is fulfilled and passionate, and he uses up every minute of every working day. That said, Henry covets his fishing time with a capital C.

We head to Montana for our annual fishing trips in August, but Henry will start packing in January. Every year he does a vacation countdown. Beginning long before our scheduled departure, at least once a day he'll say something like, "Only three months, two days, and ten hours until I'm back on the river in Montana."

These cherished trips take him away from Los Angeles and New York City and his wonderful but demanding career in the entertainment industry. Sitting in a boat or standing in the river, Henry can relax and enjoy each moment. He is finally offstage and free to be just another guy chasing after trout. Surrounded by mountains, wildflowers, and nature's own cast and crew, he feels spiritually cleansed and recharged.

Henry relishes every minute on the water, every fish, every reflection and ripple, every beam of sunlight on the shoreline, and even each drop of rain on the river. He basks in the quiet and has no tolerance for anything that distracts from the wilderness experience. Fly-fishing is his bliss. And he fiercely protects his time in that world.

Henry and I had more fights on our first day fishing together than in all our previous years of marriage. Once in the boat, my mild-mannered, loving husband turned into someone else's aggressive, cranky spouse. Luckily, there was a guide between us, or one of the Winklers might have been tossed overboard.

I was stunned at this development because that first day began peacefully enough with a nice breakfast and quiet preparations. Then, when we arrived at the put-in point, Henry, without a word, commandeered the front seat of our boat. I was taken aback by this power play.

The bow seat on the boat is considered the best in the house because it puts you in position to be the first to cast into undisturbed waters populated by unwary fish. I would have gladly given up that coveted seat to my husband, but he didn't ask. He just seized it.

Even worse, once we were on the river and ready to fish, Henry proceeded to completely disregard fly-fishing etiquette by madly casting into my waters as well as his own. His fly invaded my fishing space time and time again. He tangled my line, disturbed my fish, and slapped the water loudly.

I was shocked. My husband is normally one of those rare men who opens and holds every door and always pulls out my chair at dinner. He is a perfect gentleman in every social situation. But, as I discovered, these rules of etiquette do not apply on the river.

Henry was so crazed on that day we spent in the same boat—

seven long hours—that ever since then, we have fished in separate boats with separate guides, in separate places on the river. We do sometimes meet for a picnic lunch, but Henry views these breaks as interruptions from his time with the fish.

The guides usually caution other people to stay clear of Mr. Winkler's boat, especially if he has just arrived at freshwater. It's very hard for Henry when people recognize him on the river and want to chat. They spot him, even with a hat, glasses, and his nose covered with zinc oxide. He is always too nice to say "Please keep moving," but believe me, that—or worse!—is what he's thinking.

Henry becomes very territorial on the river. He recently admitted that when he sees water that looks "fishy," a strange spirit comes over him and demands that he cast his fly into that area. He claims it is an unconscious and overwhelming urge beyond his control, and he doesn't want anyone else fishing in that spot.

It's also true that Henry never forgets where he saw a fish. He'll come back three years later to a spot where he saw a big Brown Trout, hoping it's grown even bigger and is finally hungry for his fly.

There are other odd Henry behaviors unique to our Montana fishing trips. We usually stay at beautiful Firehole Ranch, where it is customary to dine with other guests. Breakfast conversation often includes sharing where each person plans to fish that day. Not so for Henry. He keeps his plans to himself because he wants to catch all the trout in Montana and contiguous states.

IT IS SO MUCH FUN WATCHING STACEY BECOME COMPLETELY
TAKEN OVER BY THE TASK AT HAND.

Other quirks appear during dinner each night in the lodge. The Zen of fly-fishing is all about the experience of being engaged and alive in the moment. You catch and release. You don't keep score. So in keeping with that spirit, most of the fly-fishermen and fisherwomen don't boast about how many trout they've caught, or how big their catches were, down to the exact pounds and length. Instead, they reflect on the beauty of the day and the joys of being in the mountains and on the river. In truth, they're a competitive bunch, but they hide it well.

Not my Henry. He will gladly provide a catch count, and he brings visual aids! Henry photographs each and every fish he's hooked, often from several angles. He proudly exhibits these daily pictorials at the dinner table, reciting the length and weight of each trout from memory.

Henry compiles this information methodically in his leather-bound Fishing Journal. Every night he notes in tiny little handwriting all the fish caught during the day. No fish fact goes unrecorded. (I think he pads his numbers just a little bit.)

Like most spouses, I have learned to adjust to my husband's quirks, although I do chide him just a little for sleeping in his waders and heading to the river at dawn in thirty-seven layers of Orvis, J. Crew, and L.L.Bean. He is so organized and methodical with his fishing outfit that he lays out each day's multilayered ensemble the night before.

This is like a religious ceremony—the arranging of the vestments. First the long underwear, then a T-shirt, then a big old flannel shirt, fishing pants, rain suit, parka, a fishing hat, socks, and waders, not to mention his lip balm, sunblock, scissors, and fishing knives. He often takes a backup set of clothes because, frankly, he tends to fall in the river a lot.

Try as I might, I can't fully explain his strange behavior. But that is my Henry, and it's his world you are about to enter. I love Henry for his amazing good nature and for his Montana mania, too. When we have our minor meltdowns, he always looks at me and says, "Through thick and thin." And I think, *If this is the only insanity in an otherwise thoughtful, wonderful man, we'll be just fine.*

Fly-fishing makes Henry happy, and those of us who love him are overjoyed that he loves it so much. We want him to be happy and fulfilled, and as you are about to discover, it is always a pleasure to be with Henry, even when he is an absolute maniac on the water.

THIS PICTURE WAS TAKEN JUST
OUTSIDE THE DINING ROOM
OF THE FIREHOLE RANCH ON
HEBGEN LAKE, MONTANA. I SEE
THIS VIEW TWICE A DAY WHILE
I'M THERE—AT BREAKFAST
AND AT DINNER. THE LIGHTING
CONSTANTLY CHANGES.

I've Never Met an Idiot on the River

THIS IS HOW I SPEND MOST OF MY TRIP IN MONTANA. YOU HAVE TO KNOW THE
LOSS IN ORDER TO APPRECIATE WHAT YOU'VE CAUGHT.

Chapter 1
Fish Out of Water

This wondrous book in your hands is a dream I thought would never happen, and it is the result of my late-blooming passions for fly-fishing and nature photography. I have the enthusiasm of a convert because nature and I did not mingle much in my childhood. I grew up in the great indoors of New York City, which included our family apartment at Seventy-Eighth and Broadway. My only hikes were to the bus stop or subway, with occasional forays into Riverside Park, where my first Schwinn bike was stolen.

We did have a summer home on beautiful Lake Mahopac, but even there, in upstate New York, I was a shut-in. My parents, Harry

Irving and Ilse Anna Maria Winkler, sentenced me to summer school for life, or so it seemed. For four straight summers, I was chained to the same basic geometry course—all to no avail. I was lost in the Pythagorean wilderness. To this day, I can't tell a polygon from polyester. (I do know that you can't wear a hypothesis.)

To say I struggled in school is an understatement. My parents and teachers labeled me as lazy, a slow learner, and an underachiever. My mother and father, both German immigrants, saw their high expectations for me laid low. They lost patience early on and made no effort to hide it, becoming very critical of me, and sometimes cruel. Their pet name for me was "dumb dog." They, of course, said it in German, which made it sound even meaner: *dumm Hund*.

Thanks to their delightful scorn and my own feelings, I spent most of my childhood with my self-esteem down around my ankles. But I was not dumb or lazy. I had undiagnosed dyslexia, a neurological disorder that affects your ability to read and write and learn word pronunciations. Dyslexia is a learning disability, and because of it, I was stuck, academically speaking, in the bottom 3 percent of American schoolkids.

I was really only bad in a few subjects, like math, spelling, history, reading, geography, geology, biology, chemistry, art, and usually gym, if it involved a ball. All right, so I was bad at every subject except lunch. (I had extraordinary tuna fish sandwich–eating abilities.) Along with my learning disability, I had trouble with hand-eye coordination. My eyes and my hands were not and are not great friends. So whatever the playground sport, I was usually among the last picked—if I was picked at all. Otherwise I was a cheerleader, complete with megaphone.

The dyslexia impacted so many things in my life, especially my self-confidence. Like I said, I had zilch. Feelings of inferiority pervaded everything I did, affecting my social life, my participation in sports, and how I viewed the world and, most importantly, my place in it.

Humor was my weapon against all these challenges. I became the class clown, the limbo dance king, and a master of improvisation and impersonations. Somehow, Henry the Underachiever managed to graduate McBurney School for boys and get into Emerson College, a very wonderful institution of higher learning, but only after taking geometry four times.

Yet I still wrestled with insecurities, even after I'd earned a bachelor's degree at Emerson and a master's from Yale School of Drama and had experienced a bit of success as a young actor on *Happy Days*. You wouldn't believe, for example, what a big deal it was for me to join the *Happy Days* softball team. I'd never been part of an organized sports team as a kid. I was on the swimming team in high school for about a week. Unfortunately, I ate breakfast before a practice and vomited in the pool. I don't know why, but I was immediately asked to leave.

To my surprise, I became the *Happy Days* team's star pitcher and a decent hitter, though never really much of a fielder. My fielding strategy went like this: If the ball was hit in my direction, I didn't put my glove out. Instead, I threw my whole self at it. For years, my entire left side was black and blue with ball-sized bruises. As a matter of fact, there were times you could see the baseball stitches imprinted in my skin. I'm not kidding.

Still, I loved being on the team with our other cast members, all of whom were good athletes. (Even Mrs. C—Marion Ross—who always found a way to get on base. She was very scrappy.) Our *Happy Days* version of the *Bad News Bears* traveled all over the world, and we had so many wonderful and unusual experiences.

My son Jed was our team's ball boy, so he accompanied us in 1983 to Japan, where we played a series of games against our American troops. It was my first trip there. Jed and I were sipping green tea on the bullet train speeding between Tokyo and Kyoto one fall day, when Anson "Potsie" Williams came running into our car and said, "Come with me. You've got to see this!"

Jed and I followed him through one car after another until we reached one filled with Japanese college students. They were a choral group headed for a competition, and they were singing away on the train. When they saw three Americans in the doorway of their car, the choir spontaneously broke out into "She'll be coming 'round the mountain when she comes."

TEAM SPORTS DID NOT COME INTO MY LIFE UNTIL I JOINED THE HAPPY
DAYS SOFTBALL TEAM. RON HOWARD, DON MOST, AND WALTER VON
HUENE TAUGHT ME TO PITCH. CATCHING WAS A WHOLE OTHER KETTLE
OF FISH.

They serenaded us as the bullet train sped through the beautiful countryside. Brilliant yellow ginkgo tree leaves rained down on the tracks as we sped past them. What a moment! I've never applauded a performance with more enthusiasm. Not even my own.

Playing on the *Happy Days* softball team was a special joy for me because I'd always assumed that athletics weren't my thing, and I was embarrassed by that. I made many false assumptions about my abilities because I didn't find out that I had dyslexia until years later. Eventually I realized that such assumptions are like termites. They eat away at professional and social relationships, adversely affecting your perceptions of the world and of yourself, as well as your ability to enjoy life to the fullest.

Happy Days really described my life during that time. With my acting and sporting successes, my self-esteem rose from down around my ankles to where it is now, somewhere around my sternum. Another major boost came when, at the age of thirty-one, I discovered why reading and writing had always been so difficult for me.

Jed was having trouble in school. Stacey and I took him in for tests to determine why this very bright and verbal kid couldn't seem to put his thoughts on paper. After a series of interviews and tests, the learning specialists diagnosed Jed with dyslexia. When they described the symptoms and causes to us, I thought, *Wow that really sounds like me, too!*

I was so relieved to finally find an explanation for my reading and writing and softball-catching challenges. But while this was very liberating news, it was not an instant fix. To my surprise, many old insecurities and fears lingered for years. Until just recently, for example, every time I was offered a new acting role, instead of feeling good about the opportunity, I'd be hit with nagging self-doubts, the same fears and insecurities: *Oh my God, why did I say yes? I don't think I know how to act anymore!*

Baggage. I had some baggage. All of my life, I had assumed certain things were beyond my capabilities, mentally and physically. Not in my wheelhouse, I'd think. Rather than risk failing or looking foolish when trying something new, I'd retreat or use humor to avoid it. I was an escape artist, until I finally figured out that if I just took on new things one step at a time, one foot in front of the other, conquering first one detail then the next, I could accomplish what I'd assumed was impossible.

Fly-fishing is one of the biggest challenges I've taken on, which is why I've come to love it so much. The beauty of the sport and the surrounding landscape inspired my interest in nature photography. And both of these newfound hobbies have led me to great new experiences and to meeting some of the nicest and wisest people on the planet.

I've made so many friends among the fly-fisher peoples of the world, including the gracious hosts, guides, and regular visitors at Firehole Ranch in Montana; the staff at Galloup's Slide Inn Fly

SOMETIMES, WHEN I STARE AT THIS PHOTOGRAPH, IT INVITES ME IN COMPLETELY, AND I AM CALMED BY THE COLORS.

Shop, where I buy my fishing license each year; and all the other fly-fishing enthusiasts I meet on and around the rivers. Each and every person I've met through this sport seems to be grounded and sensible and, well, I've just never met an idiot on the river.

Every river has an aura all its own, but most of those I've fished have a serenity that seems to wash over those who stand in the waters. This mellow feeling is shared by all of us. Fly-fishing is a sport, but it's also a form of meditation that attracts men and women from every socioeconomic level. We are bonded by our shared passion.

Fly-fishing has enriched Winkler World on many levels. I don't claim to be a master of the sport, but it's quite rewarding to do it well enough so that I have the pleasure of meeting many, and I mean many, fish face-to-face. When I first came to fly-fishing about fifteen years ago, I promptly fell in love with the physical, mental, and spiritual aspects of it, especially the sheer bliss of floating down the river immersed in nature's gorgeous gifts. Every visit since then has only deepened my appreciation of the sport and the special places it takes me, in the world and also in my head and heart.

I'm glad to share the pleasures I derive from fly-fishing with you in this book, as well as some of the lessons I've learned by venturing beyond what was comfortable and familiar to me. Yes, *Happy Days* don't have to end in high school or college or wherever you are in your life. I encourage you to use up every moment, to explore every nook and cranny that interests you, and to be adventurous.

Given my lack of street cred as an outdoorsman and the low levels of my pre- and post-Fonzie machismo, you might wonder how I came to try something as adventurous as fly-fishing. Well, I'm an actor, so naturally I blame my lawyer, Skip Brittenham III. He and his best friend, the late literary agent Leonard Hanzer, invited Stacey and me to join them on a fishing trip down the Smith River in Montana, circa 1993. We were excited by the idea, but intimidated, too. Skip and Leonard were serious and competitive fly-fishermen. They'd dipped their wading boots in the world's best trout streams, tying their own flies as they went.

Neither Stacey nor I had ever cast a line. The only trout we'd seen were those we'd ordered as entrées, usually with side salads. Fortunately, before Skip took two Hollywood greenhorns into the wilds of Montana, he gave us a few lessons in his Beverly Hills backyard. We practiced our first casts into the crystal-clear waters of his swimming pool. (No fish were injured in the making of this story.)

One of the keys to catching fish, Skip told us, is to keep your line straight on the water so you don't spook the fish before they leap up and grab the fly. You have to keep your line taut so that it runs parallel to the water surface, carrying the fly directly over the spot where you hope the fish will strike. This requires finesse and a feel for it that is learned only through practice. Skip told me hand-eye coordination was also a big factor. *Whoops! Count me out,* I thought.

It seemed so impossible at first. I had difficulty timing the cast and setting the hook once the fish took the fly. Skip grew frustrated during our first practice sessions because I was leaving too much slack line on the water. That's a bad thing because if the fish takes the fly, you can't tighten your line fast enough to create the tension needed to hold the fish on the barbless hook. If you give the fish too much slack, the trout will spit the fly out of its mouth and take off for the underwater grocery store.

This is where the traditional fly-fishermen greeting "tight lines" comes from. It also serves as a nice metaphor for my experience with this new challenge. Only after I took up the slack of my insecurities and tightened the lines of my self-confidence did I begin to get a knack for casting. I had to risk failing before I could get it right.

When I speak to young people, one of the things I tell them is that the anticipatory fear of trying something is always far worse than actually doing it. That's certainly true of acting, but I think it's equally true of scuba diving, giving a speech, or interviewing for a job. Just about anything you set out to do in the cold, cruel world looks and sounds worse before you throw yourself out there and go for it.

With fly-fishing, it wasn't any different. When I was learning to cast, my old fears of failure crept up on me. I thought of all the reasons I couldn't learn properly. But in practicing over and over, I discovered that casting was not as complicated as I'd envisioned,

THIS IS THE VERY POND IN IDAHO FALLS, IDAHO, WHERE MAX AND JED PERFECTED THEIR CASTING. AS YOU CAN IMAGINE, IT HOLDS A SPECIAL PLACE IN MY HEART.

"WHAT ARE YOU DOING, BOB?"
"I DON'T KNOW, FRANK. WHAT ARE YOU DOING?"
"LOOKIN' AT YOU, BOB."

CATCH AND RELEASE—THAT IS THE MOTTO I LIVE BY. I DON'T EVEN EAT TROUT IN A RESTAURANT.

and that when I broke the cast down into steps, there was a simple elegance to the sport. I discovered that fly casting could be learned, like dancing. You repeat the steps over and over until the movements are embedded in your muscle memory. You can learn the steps in a half hour and then perfect them for the rest of your life. With enough practice casting, I became so proficient that the herds of moose in the bushes quit snickering.

I'm still learning and working on being the best fly caster I can be. There's no kidding around when I describe my technique as U-G-L-Y. Nor am I being falsely modest. I don't have the precision or the economy of movement you see with the most graceful fly-fishing artistes. My wrist bends. My timing is off. And my line does not flutter like an elegant waterfowl as it lands on the water.

When you cast, you are supposed to bring the rod to a straight-up twelve o'clock position, so the line can load up behind you. Then you flick the rod to the two o'clock position, so the line gently floats out and lands straight on the water. I'm probably at 12:30 and then somewhere around 4:15, but thankfully, trout can't tell time. I know that because I keep catching them.

For the longest time, dry fly-fishing, in which your fly remains on top of the water, was difficult for me, but I managed to become a reasonably good wet fly fisherman, or nympher, quickly enough. Nymph flies are modeled on the insect larvae that start their lives at the bottom of the river and eventually work their way up to the surface. For a long time, I was comfortable just nymphing, casting nymphs right below the surface. Every time someone tried to convince me to try a dry fly, my insecurity took over, so I stuck with the wet ones.

Most beginners struggle with dry fly-fishing, and some never learn to do it because the fact is, you still can catch a lot of fish by nymphing. I discovered, though, that with a little courage and a lot of practice, dry fly-fishing could be mastered. And it's worth the effort. There is no bigger thrill than having a gorgeous trout leap up and grab your fly atop the water. An electric charge runs up your line and pole and through your entire body. But you have to remain calm, set the hook, tighten your line, and play the fish without releasing it too early. It's great fun!

Rowan Nyman, a talented guide at Firehole Ranch who fishes 280 days a year and spends each winter tying two thousand flies, has worked with me over the last couple of years, teaching me how to dry fly-fish. He's the reason I've progressed so far. Now about 90 percent of my fishing is with dry flies. And my self-esteem is almost up to my neck.

I am an optimist by choice. I always believe my cup is half full, rather than half empty. But I'm also a realist, and I thought I was being realistic by doubting my ability to become a good dry fly-fisherman. Instead, I have become a very enthusiastic and not too shabby fisher-person.

EVERY YEAR SINCE 1996, I HAVE PASSED UNDER THIS BRIDGE ON THE MADISON RIVER IN MONTANA. ONE DAY, I TOOK A PICTURE AND REALIZED THAT THERE IS BEAUTY IN EVERYTHING.

I'm a late bloomer when it comes to fly-fishing. But the feeling of growth and the sense of accomplishment that have come with this activity have helped me stretch and grow in other areas of my life. My increased self-confidence has helped me to be a better actor, a better husband, a better dad, and a better person.

Because fly-fishing gave me such a boost, I worked up the courage to write the Hank Zipzer book series with my partner, Lin Oliver. Those books have been read by millions of kids around the world. With seventeen volumes to date, our series is designed to encourage children to develop their gifts and passions and never let anyone else's labels or opinions limit their lives. You know I've been down *that* road, and I'd like to help as many kids as possible avoid it. One out of five children has some sort of learning difficulty and has to struggle like I did, but I tell them that they can achieve their dreams, just as I've done.

People tell me that my work on the *Royal Pains* television series is some of the most relaxed acting I've ever done. I believe my comfort in my role on the show as Eddie Lawson has to do with the self-confidence I've gained out on the river. My only regret is that I didn't pick up a rod and reel earlier in life. Think of all the other trout I could have pestered! And think of how relaxed I'd be as an actor; I could play comatose patients like nobody's business!

Relaxing wasn't easy for me until I stepped off the plane and shook hands with Montana for the first time. The mountains and rivers of Big Sky Country are my easy chair. I'd read somewhere that the sound of rushing water at eighty decibels is the most soothing sound to mankind, and, yes, I have found that to be so true. My first time on the river, surrounded by snow-covered peaks and the big, blanketing blue sky, I felt as if my brain were afloat. Being on the river is almost a religious experience. It's like being in church, only with mayflies instead of hymnals.

My family was inspired to buy me a nice camera on that first meeting with Montana, and whenever I wasn't fishing, I was photographing. (Okay, sometimes I did both at the same time.) This book, then, features a few of the gazillion photographs I've taken on my fishing trips. The publisher wanted to include some of my actual trout, too, but I am a catch-and-release fisher-guy, and besides, I'm told most bookstores lack a freezer section.

Still, I hope you will enjoy this modest book. But mostly, I hope my stories will inspire you to tighten up your own lines of self-confidence, toss your doubts and fears to the wind, and do whatever it is that you've always wanted to do. You won't regret it, I promise.

IF ONLY WE REALLY COULD REACH UP AND TOUCH THE SKY.

Chapter 2
The River Is a Washing Machine for My Brain

Recorded in August 2010 at Firehole Ranch, Montana

It's 3:15 in the afternoon.

Fishing is done.

I feel every muscle in my upper body.

What a wonderful day.

Talk about contentment.

*I took the fly off my rod and put it on my hat with the rest of
my collection.*

There are teenagers in river rafts going down the river.

Boys and girls. I'd say they're sixteen, seventeen years old.

There's a little boy about five years old sitting in the middle of
* one raft.*

They're all connected.

And the boys are showing off for the girls, as happens on this
* wonderful planet.*

Diving backwards off the raft, doing somersaults into the river.

Wow-ee.

Just wow-ee. How joyous to be alive and on the river!

My heart lives in New York, where I was born and raised.

My body lives in Los Angeles, where I do much of my work.

My soul lives in Montana, where I fish.

I am most at peace on a river in Montana. I liken the experience to
a washing machine for my brain. Being there is transforming. While
under the Big Sky, I am only concerned with fishing and catching. If
you allow your mind to wander anywhere else, you will neither catch
nor land your trout.

In Montana I am so focused on fishing that my mind is cleared of
everything else. Catching trout is on my brain from the time I break
out my rod and reel and start practicing my casts in the driveway at
home until I leave Montana at the end of each trip.

CATCHING A BEAUTIFUL BROWN TROUT GIVES YOU A FEELING THAT IS INDESCRIBABLE. AND BELIEVE ME, I HAVE TRIED TO PUT IT INTO WORDS.

SOMETIMES, WHEN YOU'RE SITTING IN A BOAT
ON THE RIVER, YOU COME AROUND A BEND,
AND YOUR HEART SKIPS A BEAT WHEN YOU
SEE THE EXPANSE LAID OUT IN FRONT OF
YOU LIKE GOD'S CARPET.

I've been known to choke up while departing Montana because I am so fond of Firehole Ranch, owner Lyndy Caine, and all the people we've connected with in that great place over the years. They include Bruno Georgeton, the master chef, and his wife, Kris, the master baker, who have been there for as long as Stacey and I have been going. We are so at home there that whenever it's time to leave the ranch and end our vacation, gratitude overcomes me. I'm grateful for how spectacular it is, and I realize how fortunate I am to spend time in such an incredible place.

When I return home from Montana, I'm always glad to be back among my children and our dogs, Charlotte and Linus. But I miss the river: the tranquility, the peace, the refurbishing of the soul that only happens there for me.

Once I leave behind the rivers and mountains, something else happens: Every bit of Montana Zen drains out my toes and away from my body, to be replaced by thoughts of paying the mortgage, the leak in my shower, or the pile of scripts that need reading. Good-bye Paradise. Back to business.

Here's hoping you have a similar place you can't wait to visit and never want to leave. If you don't have your own Montana, I urge you to find one. For me, visiting Montana is like having a back adjustment. I feel all out of whack when I'm not there, and fragments of my life crack back into place once I arrive. It's a great place to solve a problem and soothe hurt feelings.

Not to sound like a tourist brochure, but Montana is not just a state; it's another state of mind. I love the rugged surroundings, and thanks to the wonders of long underwear, flannel shirts, and fleece jackets, I've even made peace with the nippy chill of August mornings. I've also warmed to the challenge of fly casting, thanks to the sense of accomplishment I find in landing a beautiful trout. I especially savor the moment when I place the fish back in the water, thank it, and send it home again.

I lose myself and all sense of responsibility in Montana. You realize in those majestic surroundings just how insignificant you really are. Yet, at the same time, you realize just how connected you are to every other person and thing.

Looking at a box of artificial flies, for example, I silently thank the person who, hundreds of years ago, first figured out that the best way to catch fish was to create lures that resembled the nymphs and flies off a fish's favorite menu—those tiny insects that are hatched in the water and then emerge from it, living on the surface and flying above it before returning to the water to mate and die.

Since those first artificial flies were created, hundreds upon hundreds of variations have been crafted, giving us the Parachute Adams, Prince Nymph, Pheasant Tail, Hare's Ear, Woolly Bugger, Copper John, Dahlberg Diver, and Royal Wulff. And now the world has the Winkler, my very own personal fly, which was created for me by Tommy Thompson of Chattanooga, Tennessee. I met the

THIS IS THE PART OF
THE RIVER WHERE YOU
HAVE TO WADE. NO
BOATS ALLOWED. AS
YOU STAND IN THE RIVER
BRACING YOURSELF
AGAINST THE RUSHING
WATER, YOU CAN TRULY
UNDERSTAND THE
POWER OF THE RIVER.

Thompson family while speaking at a university there. Tommy was a passionate and talented fly fisherman, and we connected immediately over our shared love of the sport. A few weeks after I returned home, a small box arrived in the mail. The box was filled with handcrafted white parachutes with wings—size 14 flies. I put them to the test at the very next fishing opportunity. They were highly successful. Sadly, Tommy passed away after a long and courageous battle with cancer. I keep his wonderful handmade Winkler flies in their box in his memory.

Tommy was as avid about making flies as he was casting them, and he was not alone in his passion. I have heard that some fly makers scuba dive along the river bottoms of Montana just to see just what is living down there so they can bring their handcrafted flies closer to perfection. Through this passionate tradition, all the generations of fly-fishing aficionados are connected to each other and to these fly craftsmen, just as those who play piano concertos can trace the roots of their music to the first piano makers and composers of classical music.

Fly-fishing has helped me reconnect to all that is around me by putting me back in touch with the natural world, which feeds my own natural instincts. Because of my work, I live part of the time in New York City and mostly in Los Angeles. To survive in large cities, sometimes you have to tune out all the noise and chaos around you. On the river, though, I tune in once again to all five senses, as well as to my gut instincts. You have to pay attention to all that you hear, see, touch, taste, and smell in the wilderness, and you have to act on your intuition if you are going to catch any fish.

This really hit home with me on a fly-fishing trip fifteen years ago. I was with my son Max, who was twelve years old at the time. We were in Montana, this time at a lodge owned by director and screenwriter David Ondaatje, who is, among other things, the nephew of Michael Ondaatje (the author of *The English Patient*) and the owner of the legendary R.L. Winston Rod Company in Twin Bridges, Montana.

A blue-ribbon stream, the Beaverhead River, runs through David's property. One evening Max and I went out for the night hatch. David, a wonderful fisher-person himself, served as our guide, which was a good thing because once the sun went down, I couldn't see my own feet. "Listen for the fish," David said. Since he is a native of Canada, I thought at first that he was giving me the sort of cryptic stage direction known only to Toronto thespians. Not knowing how else to respond, I did as I was told. I listened, and lo and behold, for the first time in my life, I heard the wondrous sound of fish slurping! They were night feeding on the last hatch of bugs for the day.

"Cast your line out there where the fish are feeding!" David instructed.

My son became my personal cheerleader and coach at that point: "C'mon, Dad, you can do it! This is great!"

JED IS A GOOD FISHERMAN. AND IT'S VERY IMPORTANT TO HIM
THAT ALL HIS FISHING GEAR IS UP TO DATE.

Since I always do EXACTLY what my directors, guides, and sons tell me, I cast blindly into the inky trench of the river, toward the fishy slurps. Instantly, something took the fly. I could feel it was a good-size fish, and it turned out to be an eighteen-inch trout. Ten seconds earlier, I had no idea this fish was even in the same zip code.

There was not a single beam of moonlight. I caught that lovely trout purely on Winkler sonar alone. What a wonderful experience that was! What a wonderful feeling. I'd accomplished something rare in the world of sports and certainly rare in the world of me. It's something you never forget. Even as I write about it now, it makes me smile.

Even better, I did it with Max cheering on his dad. I'll never forget that moment: the darkness, the sound of the fish feeding on swarming insects, and especially the cheers from my son, which were like echoes of all the encouragement Stacey and I had given him and his brother, Jed, and sister, Zoe, over the years.

That moment is on my life's highlights reel. I seem to have more of those magical moments in Montana than anywhere else. Being there allows me to be present and to savor all that occurs as it occurs.

I mean, where else would a guy hear a fish slurp? And where else would you hear the heartfelt sincerity in a son's encouragement of his father?

When I fish in the busy silence of a Montana river, I am grateful time and again for the gifts that come with listening, not just with the ears but with the heart and soul. In the terrific book and movie

A River Runs Through It, one of the characters says that the only way to hear God's voice is to listen to it in the river. I think there are many other places where you can hear God's voice, but the river is surely one of them.

Whenever I'm on a river, I marvel at nature's plan. There are purple and yellow flowers on the Montana riverbanks that you can't find along the rivers in the Amazon or in Switzerland. This confirms for me that there is a Plan, a wonderful, thoughtful Plan that we must be careful not to ruin.

On the river, I'm reminded also that when I am truly quiet, I hear not what I'm thinking or expecting, but what is there to be heard. One of the most valuable lessons I've learned as a parent is that if you really listen, you can hear what your children truly need rather than what you want to give them. The same applies to listening to the director. Acting is reacting and responding to the situation and to your fellow actors and the script provided.

Active listening is the secret art at the center of all experience. You have to be quiet and open, not just quiet. At one point in my life, I thought this was a unique truth that I'd discovered but, to my dismay, I came to realize it is a bit of wisdom passed down through the ages in many different forms by many different voices and to many different listeners. As I've grown older, I've accepted that being original is not nearly as important as being aware; the revelation, the epiphany, is the thing.

But it's not just about listening to the world or to others. Listening to yourself—to your own intuition and instincts—is equally important. The best fly fisher-folk cast to where they know the fish will next appear. They don't have a sixth sense. They have a fish sense. Their sonar picks up fins in motion, and they hone in.

After all these years of trying hard to become a better fisher-folk, I have come to rely on my intuition about where the fish will be lurking. I trust my gut. One of the rules of life I picked up somewhere is that your head knows some things, but your stomach knows everything. Every time I've violated that rule and second-guessed my gut instinct, I've been smacked in the mouth with a two-by-four.

Oh, you want an example, do you? *Turner & Hooch*! Need I say more? I was hired to be the director of that movie and my gut told me not to do it, but I overruled the aforementioned gut and thirteen days into filming, I was fired. It was a horrible, horrible moment in my career and in my life.

I didn't recover from being fired for the longest time. Overcoming that feeling of rejection was a lesson in itself, but the greatest lesson was buried in the experience. It was learning to trust my intuition and not second-guess myself. I knew when I first read the *T&H* screenplay that I should not take the directing job. I just couldn't resist because it was a feature film for Disney. I was enchanted by the Disney magic—all that pixie dust and Mickey Mouse stuff—instead of listening to my gut.

HEBGEN LAKE, MONTANA,
AT ABOUT FIVE O'CLOCK IN
THE AFTERNOON.

THIS IS MAX, HOOKED UP WITH A BROWN TROUT IN THE POND PICTURED ON PAGE 36. LOOK AT HIS CONCENTRATION!

That's not to say that following your instincts will always bring you a big payday. I've spent many hours casting into waters I felt were promising, only to watch my fly drift unheeded while behind me I could hear my guide Rowan coaxing the fish: "C'mon, fish, take it. Take it now, you know you're hungry."

Some days, the fish don't cooperate. It's the same with acting: Some days you give a great audition for a role but you don't receive a callback. Still, when you follow your intuition and do your best, living with the not-getting is so much easier. You always have the satisfaction of having left your best in the audition room, or on the river.

Doing your best is a tremendous defense against disappointment. When you take your best shot and fail, you can pick yourself up, you can dust yourself off, and you can always start all over again, filled with hope.

And isn't that what fishing—and life—are all about?

I HAVE NO IDEA WHY, BUT I AM MOVED BY REFLECTIONS. IT DOESN'T MATTER IF THE REFLECTION IS IN A WINDOW, THE WATER, OR A PUDDLE. THIS WAS TAKEN AT EIGHT O'CLOCK IN THE MORNING ALONGSIDE THE HIGHWAY WE TAKE TO GET TO THE MADISON RIVER IN MONTANA.

Chapter 3
Point, Push, and Pray

My adventures in nature photography began many, many years ago when Stacey, Jed, and I were vacationing at Jenny Lake Lodge in Grand Teton National Park. Like most tourists in the area, I was awestruck by the beauty of the mountains, rivers, and forests.

One day we wandered into nearby Jackson, Wyoming, a beautiful mountain town. We were walking through its charming downtown shopping area, when I was drawn to a photography gallery called Light Reflections, which was owned by the happily named Frederic Joy.

Mr. Joy was not only a very good photographer but also a terrific businessman. He'd set up shop in the absolutely perfect place for selling nature photos to enraptured tourists. But really, he didn't have to sell me a thing. I sold myself, for Joy, for Joy!

I spotted a beautiful photograph that captured the natural wonders surrounding us—snowcapped mountains, purple flowers, and a lustrous lake—all in one frame for only three hundred dollars plus tax, shipping, and handling. And I bought it.

Later I wondered about that purchase. I wouldn't say I had buyer's remorse because that wonderful photograph bought from Mr. Joy makes me a happy Henry to this day, many years later.

Still, a few days after it arrived at our Los Angeles home, the thought did occur to me that maybe I, too, could take a framable photograph in a place as gorgeous as Grand Teton National Park, one that I would enjoy looking at again and again.

I asked myself, "Do you, Henry, think you can take a picture that would please you enough to have it hang in your own home?"

"Why yes, I believe I can!" replied me, myself, and I. (I have these conversations with myself quite often—very enlightening.)

And with that, my adventures began as an aspiring nature photographer, as opposed to a family photographer. Prior to that revelation, I had spent most of my photo time snapping pictures of Stacey, Jed, Max, Zoe, and the Winkler puppies at home or on vacation.

But from that day forward, the sun was not allowed to set on either the right or left Teton without my camera capturing the moment. No prairie dog or flowering plant was safe from this zealous shooter.

Sometimes I wonder if my dyslexia plays a role in my fascination with photography. Dyslexics are challenged when it comes to processing visual information, so the desire to capture and study images would seem like a natural response to that, don't you think? I just know that photography feels natural to me. I enjoy the luxury of studying my pictures. I see something fresh and exciting in each of them every time I look at my photos.

I've learned that many famous and not-so-famous photographers had dyslexia. Mr. Ansel Adams, the legendary landscape and nature photographer, for instance, is believed to have been dyslexic.

Mr. Adams and I also share a few other things. He, too, was a big fan of the vistas at Grand Teton National Park and, oddly enough, Mr. Adams also knew Frederic Joy, who studied photography with him. And, like me, the great Ansel Adams started his adventures in photography with a very small camera. His was a Brownie. Mine was a pocket camera, until Stacey and the kids took up a collection for my birthday one year and presented me with a more sophisticated Minolta with removable lenses.

Even so, my amateur status was never in jeopardy.

To this day, I have never turned a knob or pushed a button other than the shutter on my camera—ever! I just can't figure out what the other knobs and buttons mean, even though I sleep with the manual under my pillow.

WHILE I'M CASTING FROM THE BOAT ON THE MADISON RIVER IN MONTANA, I LOOK UP, AND THIS IS WHAT I SEE.

With many years and thousands of photographs under my belt, I still stick to the basic three *P*'s of photography:

1. *Point.*
2. *Push.*
3. *Pray.*

Serious photographers will be delighted to know that my favorite shutter speed is Automatic. An f-stop, to me, is a station on the subway to Brooklyn (I think). The only technical adjustment I've ever made over the years was to the focal length of a lens.

There is no doubt in my mind that there are millions of photo people out there with more training, talent, and skill than I have— photographers who have taken classes and studied the technical aspects of the craft. Me? Aside from enjoying nature, my interest in photography is purely in the product, not the process. The photos I take are dictated by my instinct. I usually snap off three shots of the same subject: very close, a little wider, and then the widest my lens will go.

I'm a self-taught photographer, and I couldn't teach myself a thing beyond the basics. For instance, even though I began taking photos in the days when die-hard photographers made their own prints, I was totally in the dark about darkrooms. Back when I was still shooting negatives, I took my film to Harry's, a camera shop in Studio City.

WHEN I LOOK AT THIS PICTURE, I CAN ALMOST HEAR LEWIS AND CLARK FINDING
THEIR WAY ACROSS THE COUNTRY. OR A WAGON TRAIN TRYING TO GET TO CALIFORNIA.
I PICTURE A MARRIED COUPLE SITTING HIGH ON THE WAGON BENCH, STARING
STRAIGHT AHEAD, WONDERING WHETHER THEIR DREAMS WILL COME TRUE.

THIS IS ONE OF MY
FAVORITE PICTURES. IT
WAS TAKEN AFTER A
RAINSTORM. A PUDDLE
HAD FORMED ALONGSIDE
THE TRAIL MY GUIDE
ROWAN AND I TAKE DOWN
TO THE MADISON RIVER
IN MONTANA. EVERYBODY
SEES SOMETHING
DIFFERENT IN THE
FRAME. SOMEBODY EVEN
THOUGHT IT WAS THE
SURFACE OF THE MOON.

They made contact sheets for me so I could pick out my favorite shots and order five-by-seven and eight-by-ten glossy prints. Sometimes I would crop them myself using a grease pencil and a cutter, which was about as photo-geeky as I got.

Still, I became a film purist. When digital cameras were introduced, I heartily vowed "Never!" (*Note to self: Stop with the Never!*) I was such a film-o-phile that I'd take forty rolls on vacation and snap every frame. Then, once the contact sheets were made, I'd bring them home and our entire family would vote on which photos were worth printing. The voting didn't take long. Often there were only six or seven keepers from a trip.

Eventually I realized there were certain advantages—not to mention substantial savings—with digital photography. "Film, schmilm," I said. With a new gift of a Nikon COOLPIX from my wife, I became a digital convert. (So much for *Never!*) Today, I am even friends with the digital Picasa photo-editing software, but our dealings are limited mostly to clicking on the "crop" icon (much cleaner than the old grease pencil) or, my favorite, the "I feel lucky" icon.

The great thing about digital photography is that I can take as many photos as I want without lugging forty rolls of film to the river, where they might fall in, as I tend to do. Whether I'm shooting with a digital camera or film, I love capturing images that touch me emotionally and, as I said, instinctively. I click merrily away, later deleting all photographs but the ones I want to savor, or those with

THIS IS A VIEW OF MONTANA'S QUAKE LAKE, WHICH WAS CREATED BY AN ENORMOUS EARTHQUAKE ON AUGUST 17, 1959. THESE TREES ALWAYS REMIND ME OF SOLDIERS STANDING GUARD. THE LAKE IS FILLED WITH BEAUTIFUL AND PLUMP RAINBOW TROUT, USUALLY ABOUT SIXTEEN INCHES LONG.

MONTANA IS KNOWN AS BIG SKY COUNTRY. EVERYWHERE YOU LOOK, THE POWER AND SERENITY OF OUR PLANET SURROUNDS YOU.

an emotional value. I think of my photographs as visual take-home food: little tastes of Montana to tide me over until I can return to the great West.

As you can see in the photographs I've included here, reflections are one of my favorite images. I'm not sure why, but I am intrigued by their imperfect symmetries—the way patterns are often repeated but slightly altered in reflection. I hadn't realized how drawn I was to photographing reflections until my first shots came back from the developer, and I saw how many reflective ponds, pools, rivers, and lakes I'd photographed.

There is also something so compelling about looking into a simple puddle and seeing a reflected building or a stormy sky spring up at you. I've been known to blow up my puddle portraits to sixteen-by-twenty-four prints and hang them on the walls of our home.

Some people disdain puddles on the wall. I'm of a different mind!

My critics—nearly all of whom have been claimed as exemptions on the family tax return at one time or another—seem to feel I am overly fond of photographing fish. Not just any fish, but those lucky enough to be caught by me.

I plead guilty by reason of fin-sanity.

I'm crazy for fly-fishing and even crazier for fish catching, but most importantly, I'm for fish releasing. I am an avid trout fancier because they are so beautifully colored and patterned. Trout are majestic—like the Tetons, only scaled down to eighteen inches.

WHILE BROWSING THROUGH THE PICTURES FOR THIS BOOK, IT HIT ME THAT THE REFLECTION IN THE LAKE AND THE REFLECTION IN THE PUDDLE (TOP) ARE QUITE SIMILAR. THE LINES COMING OFF THE TELEPHONE POLE, THE POLE ITSELF, AND THE TREES IN MONTANA'S QUAKE LAKE SEEM TO HAVE THE SAME FEELING.

BREAKFAST! STACEY AND I ARE WAITING FOR PANCAKES AND BACON.
NOT TALKING MUCH . . . THINKING ABOUT THE DAY'S FIRST HOOKUP.

NOTE TO SELF: WHEN YOU'RE BACK IN THE CITY SITTING IN
TRAFFIC, REMEMBER HOW HAPPY YOU CAN BE.

I've been known to catch sixty trout in one day, and before I release them I record the length and weight of each one in my Fishing Journal. I also photograph each trout before saying "Thank you," and placing it back in the river to swim another day.

I carry my journal and my favorite fish photos everywhere, along with photos of my family and dogs. I am known to be quite unabashed about showing my fish portraits to anyone, at any time, in any place. I share them with fellow fisher people in Montana, with fellow actors and actresses in Hollywood and New York, with total strangers, and sometimes even with potted plants and statues in the park.

My fish photos are stored on my cell phone, stashed in my carry-on luggage, hanging on the walls at home, and lined up on every bookshelf and mantle. Some are duplicates. I don't care. Every time my eyes fall upon these photos, the feeling is always, always exquisite. I love them all. My family loves them, too, because they know how important fly-fishing and my trout are to me.

The very best thing about my photographs, though, is that everywhere I look, I am reminded of my friend, the river.

FALL IS MY FAVORITE
SEASON. THE COLORED
LEAVES COMBINED
WITH THE SOUND
OF THE RUSHING
WATER CREATE, FOR
ME, A RELIGIOUS
EXPERIENCE.

Guide   Mark & Jackie P

WATER CONDITIONS	SIZE	SPECIES	COMMENTS
Liveable / then large ones		BASS, Lincod, Coho & chinook, 11, 10, 13 2 Halibut 42, 12, 55	The Largest fish of my life - 38½ long 35 deep 42 pound chinook.
21 fish from 9" - 15" Cut throughts cut Bow Rainbows Browns & one White -	✳	BROWN TROUT Biggest 24" 6 lbs - TROUT & my life.	I felt Joyous - and grateful. I caught a 10" brown asked Zonan say can I catch the mom or dad a second later this one came on ___
and no other fish Rose to me changed to Nymphs -	went to the meadows a 3 dollar Semi dry fly	___ 17, 16, 16, 17 Browns and 14 Rainbow -
Caught one fish and we left to water.	Reynolds Bridge	Caught - 3 17 Browns -
a 21 inch Brown 4/lbs — The fish of the Day			
Rainbos on days - a Spruce moth - floated Lynns to windy foam hopper.			

Chapter 4
Casting for Joy

Recorded in August 2010 in Idaho on Henry's Fork, a tributary of the Snake River

Hi.

So here we are.

It is Sunday morning.

It is about ten o'clock.

10:04 to be precise.

We're in Idaho.

We have come to the Henry's Fork.

The Warm River flows into the Henry's Fork.

And it looks to me like there are two or three boats ahead of us
*   that are putting in.*
There's not a cloud in the sky.
The sun is unbelievable.
Shining brightly.
And the water is calling me.
I wish it were the fish calling me.

The adventure begins.
Of course, the first part of the fishing vacation is putting your
*   rig together.*
Organizing it.
Checking that the parts of the rod have been fitted together
*   well.*
You have to make sure that all the stripping guides are perfectly
*   aligned, that the new line has its leader, that you know what*
*   fly you're going to use first.*

My guide, Rowan, and I chat about this as the boat is being
*   readied to slip into the water.*
We're starting out with a hopper, a rubber-legged fly that has a
*   dropper nymph off the back.*
So we have a fly on the water and for backup—always have to
*   have backup—we have the rubber-legged stone fly that will*

HERE'S THE DREAM I HAVE EVERY DAY—THAT I AM
STANDING IN THE RIVER.

sink below the surface. Yes, it's probably a great thing to know your flies.

But I don't have to, because I have the master with me, Rowan, who knows everything there is to know about fishing on this planet, or any other.
And a little chipmunk just ran by along the bank.
So we share all this beauty with the wildlife, large and small.

Wait a second! There are two golden eagles circling above the river, looking for breakfast.
Wow-ee!
I am grateful to be alive.
I am GRATEFUL to be able to do this.

I'm sitting in front of the boat, filled with the anticipation of casting out the first line of the day.
The excitement of connecting with that first fish is over-whelming.
There is a hatch of mayflies, I think, right?
They are mayflies.
Yes, they are mayfly spinners, to be exact, just swirling through the air.
How do I know?

Rowan just confirmed it.

That is always a REALLY good sign because they are my trout's favorite snack.

But a cream-colored midge fly is what all the fish seem to be going for.

So, at 11:45 we change flies.

And I catch a brave little rainbow.

And when I say little, we're talking five inches.

As I pull up on the line to set the hook, this little guy flies out of the water, over the boat, off the line, and into the river on the other side.

This morning is filled with fish that size.

And it is just gorgeous here.

Every time I look up and see where I am, it takes my breath away.

Everything is still green.

It has been kind of a chilly summer.

Today is a beautiful day, in the seventies.

Sometimes I just feel the river and I are one.

And I don't mean that in any kind of cosmic way.

You juuust . . . you FEEL that there are fish and you just know

DRIVING TO BOX CANYON, MONTANA, 2007.

where they are sitting under the river's surface, waiting to
outsmart you.
And you FEEL that they're going to become one with your line.

Of course, there are those other times you feel cold.
Totally disconnected.
You have no instinct whatsoever.
And it turns out that's how it is—you pretty much get skunked.
Which I would imagine is the same thing in life.

Confidence—that CENTER of yours.
The just living,
and not worrying,
and just PRESENTING yourself.
It makes all the difference in the world—
whether it be a social situation,
or work situation,
or a fishing situation.

It is amazing how the type of energy you feel and put out
determines how successful you're going to be.
It's not just your ability, because you can have all the ability in
the world.
But if the energy that comes off of you doesn't invite the fish,

or the human being, or the job into your life . . .
you pretty much end up empty-handed.

You know, "If you will it, it is not a dream."
That is a phrase that was first said by Theodor Herzl more
than a century ago. And I have made it the cornerstone of my
life.
·

So, patience.
Patience. If you want something badly enough, you just have
to stick to it.
Tenacity is a cornerstone.
Also gratitude for what you have, and for what's coming.
And patience.
That is really everything.
There are times when you want to sit down.
You want to give up.
You can't allow that to happen.
If you really want it, you have to will it into being.
My wonderful lawyer, Skip Brittenham, once told me that if
you sit at the table long enough, or in the boat long enough,
the fish come to you.
The chips come to you.

I READ IN THE MONTANA ALMANAC
THAT THE BIG SKY BLANKETS 145,556
SQUARE MILES OF LAND. BUT THERE
ARE ONLY SIX PEOPLE PER SQUARE
MILE TO HOLD UP THAT MUCH HEAVEN.

Oh my God, he must be like five or six pounds!

A beautiful Brown.

That might be the largest Brown I ever caught in my LIFE.

No, it is. Definitely.

Oh . . . my . . . Lord.

I experienced pure joy on that morning, on the twenty-first of August, 2010, when I landed the biggest fish of my life. The fact that this occurred on a tributary of the Snake River named Henry's Fork seems appropriate, don't you think?

We were fishing a stretch between Warm River and Ashton, Idaho. I'd been blind casting with good results, but I'd been playing around with four- to nine-inch trout all morning, so I was feeling overdue for a bigger catch. I told my guide, Rowan, "I'm catching all the children. When will I catch a grown-up?"

Those words were hardly out of my mouth when an "Oh my God!" fish took my fly and pulled so hard I felt like I'd hooked an aircraft carrier. Rowan became very excited, which is something Rowan doesn't often do. My stalwart guide clambered out of our boat into Henry's Fork and then scrambled after Henry's fish, which was running off with Henry's line. (I can be very proprietary.)

Rowan shouted back at me over the river's roar, "You're playing this fish well."

I wasn't so sure. I feared the fish was playing me. This trout was a track star! I let the big guy run. Then, when he stopped to rest, I reeled in whatever line I could before he sprinted off in a furious rush. Seriously, when this monster trout made a run, he generated electricity. I could feel a zap up my hands and arms.

My boat was being tugged by this whopper, who was zigging and zagging so hard that it took all my strength to bring him to my left and then to my right. Suddenly, my fish friend found deep water. He dove like a nuclear submarine just below me and I swear I heard diving bells.

I hovered above, keeping my rod high, bringing in line as fast as I could, and after what seemed like fifteen minutes, the trout came rocketing up and leapt into the air.

Finally I saw my fish, a whale of a trout, a Brown Trout to be exact, a heart-stopper—my favorite kind! Before we'd even seen this fish, we knew it was a Brown by its strength. My guide yelled, "Stay calm, Henry!"

Easy for him to say.

"Now this is a fish! This is a great fish!" said Rowan. (He never does that!)

My guide took his net in hand and slipped it under the behemoth fish in a flash as it surfaced near the boat. But Mr. Trout, a mighty muscle with fins, was not about to surrender so easily. He leapt up, slapped the net away with a sweep of his tail fin, and darted away from two shocked and awed fishermen. My guide and my fish repeated this dance several times. And each time they did, I wanted to panic. I kept saying to myself, "Please, please don't lose this guy."

"Let him run! Let him run!" said my guide.

Instinctively, I let him run.

The King Fish was gone in a flash, taking ten miles of my line with him. I think he actually went up to Yellowstone Park and circled Old Faithful twice.

Eventually he tired. I wound the reel with a fury, winding and winding. Finally my big Brown was back within reach. Rowan slipped the net under him again, but there was just one problem. It turns out the Trout King was too big for the net! My guide did his best to get a hold of the monster, but it was hard going. Poor Rowan could hardly keep his balance on the slippery, rocky riverbed. He was trying to hold the boat in place with his elbow even as that huge fish was flapping in and out of his net.

Then, the defiant trout took it a step further and spit my fly out of his mouth. My heart dropped into my waders. I thought we were about to lose him. But trusty, agile Rowan managed to wrap half of the flapping fish with the net. One tiny slip, one millisecond more, and the trout of my dreams might have been back in the river and out of reach.

Instead he was secured, which allowed us to finally meet face-to-fish. Rowan handed the huge Brown to me with his arms held wide. I reached out and took him under the gills and tail, stretching and

THIS IS IT! THE BIGGEST TROUT OF MY CAREER—CAUGHT ON HENRY'S FORK IN IDAHO. OH MY, DOES THIS PHOTO MAKE ME HAPPY!

struggling to keep my balance, because this was one strapping fish.

Twenty-four inches long and more than six pounds!

"He's beautiful!" I said.

Just then, Stacey called out to me. She and her guide, Scott, had come down the river to meet us for lunch. They'd found us just in time to see me land the King.

She gave me a thumbs-up and yelled, "Good job, honey. You did great!"

This trout was an unbelievable catch, and to have Stacey there to witness me bringing him in was even more wonderful. But I had no idea they were watching, of course. I'd become entranced with playing this fish. I was lost in time and place, totally absorbed in the moment, using my brain, my body, and every ounce of my creativity to bring the big trout in.

To me, such moments are the definition of pure happiness. Life's best moments happen when you are totally engaged in an activity that challenges every part of your being.

Mind? *Check!*

Body? *Check!*

Spirit? *Check!*

You're all in. I've experienced this with acting, too. When you're working on the most intense and emotional scenes, you can do take after take after take, over and over again, and you never grow weary. A fire could break out on the set, but you are so engaged and in the flow that you stay in character. You are so focused that when you finally finish the scene, you have no idea that it is four in the morning and the rest of the world has gone to bed.

When you are in the flow like that, you are no longer trying, you are being. That's a good thing if you have a huge fish on the line, because there isn't time to ponder the wonder of it all. You are excited, but at the same time you must keep your wits about you. There are so many elements to the game. You must keep tension on the line, hold the rod high, and pull in slack, without ever forcing but instead allowing the fish to make a run and then taking in line as he turns and comes back at you as fast as he can.

You have to remember it isn't about overpowering the fish; it's about letting him wear himself out, keeping him on the line until you can net him and finally take a photo. I've tried other types of fishing, but none of them have the poetry of fly casting for trout. The light tackle connects you to the power of the fish and the rushing water of the river. I love a strong and tenacious fish. Not just because it's a challenge, but because I identify with its struggle against the current and the pull of the line, because my early life was such a struggle. I had to be tenacious. I had to fight for every good grade and I was always grateful for each opportunity. Tenacity and gratitude became my twin tenets for success. Tenacity takes you step by step to your dream, and gratitude never lets you become bitter along the way. A little patience sprinkled in allows you to stay in control and in the fight.

I WAKE UP EARLY MOST MORNINGS, ABOUT 5:15, AND KEEP CHECKING THE SUNRISE BECAUSE SOMETIMES IT LOOKS LIKE THIS, AND I AM FORTUNATE ENOUGH TO BE ABLE TO TAKE A PICTURE.

If a trout makes a run, you either give him line, or the fish will break it. You have to be just as smart and tough as the trout. Yet you can't "horse" the fish. You don't force the issue. It's like a valued relationship. You don't force the moments; you let them come. Actors have to take the same approach. You don't overpower the character or the script; you play it naturally and let the story unfold scene by scene.

When Rowan finally handed this trout to me, I had no language to describe my exhilaration and disbelief that I'd caught this beautiful creature. I really, really enjoyed that moment, and I felt exactly the same pleasure when I put that fish back into the river. Without hesitation, his Majesty the King Fish gave a flick of his fins and off he went.

There was a brief interlude during which I photographed my catch for posterity. I could hardly get all of him into the frame. As I took the shot I was stammering, "Oh my! Oh my!" over and over again. I was in shock, really. I'd heard so many stories and seen so many videos with this sort of trophy trout as the prize catch, and now I was living my own very happy ending, at the very end of my rod and line. For me, fly-fishing isn't about capturing or conquering or owning the fish. It's about sharing a moment in time with a wild creature, feeling its power and merging with its life force for just a brief period. I release my fish so that others might have the pleasure of engaging with them. And I always express gratitude for the moments we had together. I never eat them because they are too majestic and beautiful. (I would never eat a labradoodle, either, by the way.) I want all of my trout to live on so we can play again one day.

When I let my trophy trout go, there was no feeling of regret. The circle was complete. He swam away strong and healthy and prepared to fight another day. And I went back to fishing. I hope to see him on the river again soon.

Water Conditions	Size	Species	Comments
Clearish	X	X	No helicopter. Rain Fog Wind + No fish. I

Sat on a cliff side holding onto a tree flipping the Nymph to a trout. As I pulled it in he took it and I had too much slack in the line. Joe caught 10 Rainbows — He went off with his own guide Greg. Our guide Marks brother. Hard Day. I cast 25 times in a same pool and came away with nothing. Eve cooked another great meal. In bed by 10:30. Spoke to Scot Bano about our shoot. There is always tomorrow —

times out of the water. Had another on the line for 4 mins hooked 4 or 5 times but was lucky on the rest. One only get one or 2 mountain goats today up and down the scariest trails —

and I hope we can come back — it is just so _____ here

I WROTE THESE ENTRIES DURING MY TRIP TO NEW ZEALAND WITH FLY FISHING THE WORLD. TO THIS DAY, I CANNOT BELIEVE I HAD TO HOLD ONTO A TREE STUMP FOR DEAR LIFE WHILE CASTING FOR TWO BROWN TROUT THAT WERE CRUISING THE CLIFFSIDE BELOW.

AH, YES. SHARING MONTANA TIME WITH MY SON, MAX. I'M SHARING THE MAGNIFICENT COUNTRY WE LIVE IN . . . HE'S SHARING LOUD MUSIC.

Chapter 5
Going with the Flow

My son Max was about nine years old when we took him on his first fishing trip on the Madison River in Montana. I'd hoped that Max would share my enthusiasm for fly-fishing, but as soon as he took a seat in the front of the boat, he pulled out his Walkman, plugged into it, and put his feet up on the bow.

I didn't say anything to Max, and I tried not to be disappointed that he wasn't interested in fishing. It's always been important to me to be more understanding of my children than my parents were of me. So I told myself to be patient and to let my son enjoy the trip his way. Perhaps he will want to fish later. Maybe he will actually pick up a rod and, by some miracle, cast a line.

As we floated down the river, I was glad to see Max take out his earplugs and turn to our guide, Jim, a very helpful and professional fellow, who always has the right tool or piece of gear when you need it. I was hoping Max would ask Jim for a fishing tip, a lesson on how to use the rod and reel.

Instead he said, "I'm hungry."

Jim, being Jim, quickly produced a bite-sized Milky Way bar and handed it to Max. I had neglected to warn our guide that my son was hypersensitive to sugar. Giving Max even a tiny candy bar was like putting high-octane racing fuel in a go-kart.

Eight minutes later, my son was standing up in the front of our fishing boat, belting out the entire score of *Les Miserables*, his favorite musical.

I'm fairly certain Jim had never seen or heard anything quite like this, nor had the cows and moose along the river. All creatures big and small were quite stunned. I swear I saw a bear's jaw drop in shock and a fish fall out! Jim was so unnerved, his eyes resembled those gag glasses with the eyeballs dangling on Slinkys—they were practically shooting in and out of his head. He could not believe what Max was doing to the serenity of his river valley.

Jim gave me a pleading look, hoping I might pull the curtain down on Max's riverboat show.

All I could do was shrug, as if to say, "Sorry, nothing we can do until Max burns through the Milky Way galaxy."

Resignation passed over our guide's face. He stopped rowing, turned to me, and said, "At least he has a good voice, doesn't he?"

By then the boy, fueled by bits of gooey caramel, chocolate, and nougats, had moved on to selections from *Phantom of the Opera*.

A wave of crankiness rose up in me, but I chose to let it wash away. Jim would have a funny story to tell at the next river guide convention, I told myself. And Max was enjoying himself immensely. Besides, the trout did not seem to mind.

At least Max came along for the ride, I thought as I returned to blithely fishing in the back of the boat.

There were few others on the river, but the lack of an audience didn't bother Max. My son the Phantom crooned away in the bow of our boat. Whenever someone did paddle past, I wished them "tight lines" and assured them that Max was available for hire if they wanted a singing gondolier in their boats, too.

Accepting Max's deviation from my script for the day was a big step for me. But I had learned my lesson on a prior trip to the river with my daughter, Zoe. His performance of *Les Mis* on the Madison occurred after the wader-throwing incident Stacey mentioned in her Introduction.

I am a patient person about 93 percent of the time, but that was one of those times when I was overwhelmed with impatience. And to tell you the truth, I'm not sure why. I'd given up my morning fishing

THIS IS THE VERY MOMENT ZOE REALIZED FISHING
WAS NOT FOR HER.

to ride horses with Stacey, Zoe, and Max. In return, our daughter had agreed to fish with me during the afternoon, but only as long as we kept it to half a day.

Now I have to tell you something about Zoe. You see, she dawdles. She is the best—a great dawdler at the highest level, an achievement that is attainable only by fifteen-year-old girls.

"C'mon, Zoe, we need to get on the boat," I said when we were done horseback riding. "We have only limited daylight to work with." Already she was dawdling, and while I was impressed by her dawdling prowess, I wanted to make it to the river. The fish were feeding!

More dawdling ensued. And then, to my shock, and the shock of my entire family (and most of our ancestors), the wader boot in my hand went flying across the room—not at Zoe (I had the presence of mind not to be THAT big a jerk), but still, across the room, landing against the wall, just under the window.

Zoe was horrified, then hurt, and finally, defiant. As the final phase set in, her body language gave the perfect interpretation of what is meant by the phrase "digging in your heels," defining it for all time.

"I'm not going fishing with you—EVER!" she shouted.

I panicked. *Oh, oh, now what?* Do I wait for her? Do I leave her? I wanted to go fishing in the worst way and the best way, too. But I was stuck. All year I wait for those seven days on the river! And I was so close . . . except something had happened. I still wasn't sure what, or what I needed to do to make it better. (Insert heavy paternal sigh here.)

My impatience and anger quickly peaked and then gave way to remorse and guilt. An intense father-daughter discussion ensued. I won't go into the embarrassing details, but suffice it to say, the father lost ground and then found himself deep in a hole.

Meanwhile, the river was flowing, the trout were feeding, and the sun was moving rapidly across the afternoon sky.

I begged Zoe for forgiveness. I pleaded temporary insanity. But I'd cooked my own goose with one toss of the boot. After a final sweeping apology, I turned and headed for the river.

My daughter's parting words were "You're leaving me here alone. Everyone else has plans and I have NOTHING to do!"

As I write this in the fall of 2010, I want you to know that every once in a while I still, out of the blue, apologize to my beloved schoolteacher daughter for being such a curmudgeon on that day in Montana fourteen years ago.

I was being completely impatient in a place that demands patience, with a person whom I love very much. Worse yet, I'd grown up with parents who were perpetually impatient with me, and I'd vowed to be a different kind of parent, one who would always be patient with my own children. I thought I'd broken the pattern, but in fact I'd managed to come full circle.

I'd let my emotions dictate my actions, and the result wasn't pretty. I'd become frustrated because I was trying to control my daughter, and she was resisting my efforts. The lesson I drew from that meltdown was to control those things that I can control and to let go of whatever is beyond my influence.

The ironic thing is, this little lesson improved not just my relationships but my fishing, too. The value of patience has been brought home to me many times while on the river, where bad weather, tangled lines, or trout that refuse to come out and play can easily lead to frustration. It's the same patience you need as an actor on the set waiting for things to get going. You're in the zone and a light blows, or you are waiting for another actor who hasn't come out of the trailer yet. It doesn't matter where you are; patience is required in life.

I have to remind myself of this constantly, even when I get to the river. I take so much pleasure in my time there, I've found myself resenting the fact that I have to put together my seven-piece rod, piece by piece by piece, before I can fly-fish. I resent the time lost assembling the rod, then putting my line through the eyeholes, loading the boat, mounting the oars, and parking the truck. There are so many time-consuming little details that must be tended to that it seems to take hours and hours before I can actually do what I came to do: relax on the river. In my early days of fly-fishing, I'd have to talk myself down from all the anxiety that would build up while I was preparing to cast a fly into the water.

IT'S 8:30 P.M. ANOTHER LONG DAY OF
STANDING IN THE RIVER IS DONE. WE'RE
HEADING BACK TO THE LODGE. ALL I
COULD DO WAS STARE AT THIS SHEER
BEAUTY . . . AND THEN I REMEMBERED I
HAD A CAMERA.

The Das Boot incident with Zoe opened my eyes to all of this, and to my impatience in general. Up until then, I'd thought of myself as a very patient man. I'd clearly thought wrong. I had to reprogram myself by practicing the Zen of going through each detail, getting it done in its own time. I had to remind myself of my priorities. Zoe Time was more important than trout time.

The neat thing I discovered is that we have a choice. We can choose to be cranky. Or we can choose to let go of our right to be frustrated and ticked off. We can focus on the good instead. What I learned with Zoe, I practiced later with Max.

Initially I was frustrated because my son showed little interest in fishing, and I was embarrassed by his behavior in front of our guide. But then I checked myself. *Why be ticked off? I thought. Max is just responding to the sugar rush. Jim will get over it. The fish are not frightened and, lo and behold, the Earth is still revolving around the sun, and Jupiter is aligned with Mars.*

All was right with the world and the karma of the water, so I was able to move past and give up my frustration and embarrassment and my need to control the situation. What I realized was the Zen concept that submission is power. If you don't blow into the boat of frustration's sail, the boat can't move anywhere. My wacky son was enjoying himself, so why not let him?

There is power in letting go like that, and often there are

unexpected rewards. Today Max is a USC film school graduate, a director, and a screenwriter with great promise. He has written and made a couple of films and sold one to a distributor. Still, we've discussed the possibility that if the Hollywood thing doesn't work out for him, he can always find work as a singing fishing guide in Montana.

Better yet, my children have a father who has learned to love them and accept them for who they are. They still surprise me from time to time, and I like that. As a matter of fact I look forward to those moments. Years ago I'd also tried to get Max interested in horseback riding on our Montana trips. Initially he informed me that he did not like riding atop horses and added, "I don't like the sport and I don't really like the animal, either."

I didn't try to force horses or trail riding on him, and in a very short while he decided on his own to join us on our Montana trail rides. He even wears cowboy chaps he bought at the ranch, and he has learned to like "the animal" so much that trail riding has became one of his favorite Montana activities. And that makes me an unbelievably gratified, happy dad.

I even encourage Max to sing on the trail, but I make him stick to cowboy songs.

YES, HERE I AM IN A STATE OF PURE BLISS ON THE MADISON RIVER IN MONTANA.

Chapter 6
Hooked, Soaked, and Happy as a Clam

I wandered afar from my usual Montana fishing haunts a few years ago. Expert fisherman and television host John Barrett asked me to appear in a segment of his popular long-running show, *Fly Fishing the World*. Other celebrities who have fished with John over the years include supermodel Niki Taylor, actors Liam Neeson and Kevin Costner, and rocker Huey Lewis (apparently the News do not fish).

As you might guess from the show's title, each of us casts lines in a different part of the world. My destination, I'm happy to say, was New Zealand. I took my son, Jed, a very good fly-fisherman, to one of the country's beautiful Pacific islands for the taping. We were hoping to see some hobbits since they made *The Lord of The Rings* trilogy there, but no luck.

We didn't see many fish, either. The weather was unusual for this island nation, rainy and gloomy, more Gollum than Frodo. When we didn't catch a single trout on the first day, I decided that the secret to fly-fishing in New Zealand is "never give up." That just happens to be my own secret to success in life, one that has served me well in my fly-fishing adventures, my acting career, and all my other endeavors.

So I did not give up on the fish in New Zealand, and I finally caught a very nice five-and-a-half pound trout on our second day there. I also took a little tumble for John Barrett's camera crew while walking on the rugged riverbed. I've been known to fall into the water at least once a day while fly-fishing, no matter where I am in the world. I have this magnetic attraction to river bottoms. Then again, I've been known to trip and fall in the bathtub, too.

My self-dunkings do not discriminate between countries or states. There are rivers in Idaho, Wyoming, Montana, Tennessee, and, of course, New Zealand, where I have plunged. Oh, and let's not forget Canada, where somehow my waders ended up upended and full of river water. And because I am so addicted to the sport, I can't bear to just clamber to shore, dry off, change my pants, and empty my waders. Instead I remain water-bound: standing in water, surrounded by water, covered in water, and fishing my soggy little heart out.

While gravity is cruel to me, I should note that natural laws are not the only laws involved in my fishing exploits. My fishing is also governed by Murphy's Law: "If anything can go wrong, it will." The Winkler Addendum to Murphy's Law is "while Henry is fly-fishing."

Murphy's Law seems to come into play particularly when I am casting. If there is a tree on the riverbank, hanging over the riverbank, sticking out of the river, on the other side of the river, just beneath the surface of the river, or possibly in England, my fly will find it, land on it, and lodge itself for eternity.

No spider known to man can weave a web as massively tangled as the one I can create with one simple cast of my line. As it passes from behind me, over my head, and past the bow of my boat, my line can resemble abstract art, or a train wreck, depicted in microfilament. Sometimes these entanglements stop the boat dead in the water. When this occurs, I turn most gratefully to my guide and always smile as I say, "Oh, Rowan, have I got a PROBLEM for you!"

Moving targets are also mine to hook. If there is a clump of grass, a leaf, or a mere twig floating by, my fly will snag it like a heat-seeking missile.

Henry's hooks of horror do not end there. I've also proven adept at snagging myself, my guide, and total strangers, some of whom made it abundantly clear that they did not enjoy our hookup. I once snagged my own facial cheek so thoroughly that the end of the hook went all the way through the aforementioned cheek and protruded from my mouth. I had never had the slightest desire to taste or feel what a trout tastes and feels when hooked, but after that experience, I can say unequivocally that it is not the least bit enjoyable.

Since a fly-fishing hook is not barbed, the age-old, time-tested process for removing it from human flesh is to yank it out with the help of fly-fishing line and a steady hand. When I caught my cheek, my guide came to the rescue. He told me this procedure would not hurt, and I wanted desperately to believe him. My intention was to be manly and brave. That was my intention, but not, in fact, what happened.

Winkler whimpers echoed through the woods. Still, thanks to my guide, unhooked I was. This was not an experience I would ever wish to reenact, though it did give me the right to say forevermore that not only do I practice catch and release, but also catch and release has been practiced on me.

My fishing follies are a show that never ends. I fish, therefore I snag. And I go splash so often Stacey has asked me to wear water wings. Still, no matter how many times I go down, I always come bobbing back up. Tenacity is another tool in my reel. Like anyone else, I've had my ups and downs, but my determination has served me well in fishing and in life.

In speeches to schoolchildren, teachers, and other groups, I often quote author Theodor Herzl, who wrote, "If you will it, it is not a dream." (I'm fond of that quote, as you may have noticed.) I read his

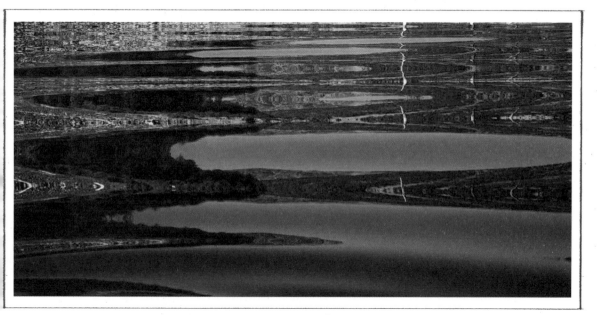

THIS REMINDS ME OF THE HAND OF NATURE, WITH ITS FINGERS REACHING OUT ACROSS MONTANA'S QUAKE LAKE.

words for the first time decades ago, and they resonated with me. I still keep that saying on display in my office for inspiration.

Believing that my dreams could become my reality is a cornerstone of my life. Each of us has to take responsibility for preparing and striving, to the best of our abilities, to make our dreams into our realities. Staying committed to this idea has allowed me to do so many things and to overcome so many obstacles. And I hope that by sharing my experiences, I can inspire others not to be intimidated and to move ever forward toward their dreams.

Somehow I knew this, even at a young age. My dyslexia had made me insecure and fear ridden as a child, but I managed to overcome those fears of failing and being ridiculed. Mostly what kept me alive during those years was determination. I was one determined kid. My grade school principal once said I needed to focus so I could be a better reader. So focus I did, or at least I tried. I bought every neon yellow highlighter in Manhattan and, as I read my schoolbooks, I highlighted every letter, every word, and every sentence.

In world history class, I highlighted the entire Middle Ages. In other classes, I highlighted the U.S. Constitution, the *Iliad*, AND the *Odyssey*. My hands glowed neon yellow at night. I was that focused. But after all that highlighting, I had no idea what I had just read. For me, that defines the word FRUSTRATION.

My struggles with learning continued despite my valiant efforts. I once earned a C and declared that day a national holiday and threw myself a party. The only thing I couldn't do was get a new stamp approved to commemorate it.

Thankfully I had some wonderful teachers, including Donald Rock and Michael Sicilian at McBurney School for boys in Manhattan. It was a tough school, very rigorous academically. We wore blue sport coats and ties and sang Gregorian chants. (I was heavily advised to lip-synch from the eighth grade on. When my voice changed, it left my body. When I sang, it sounded like the dying quacks of a mortally wounded duck.)

Mr. Rock saw that my self-esteem was low because of my poor grades and my inability to chant in key. I took a lot of flak, some of it in Latin, which I didn't understand. One day he told me something that made a huge difference in my life. He said, "I promise you, Henry, when you get out of here, you will be fine."

Mr. Rock was my rock. He was that rare adult who believed in me, and his confidence in me was contagious. I made it out of McBurney and through high school, mostly thanks to drama class and theater productions and great teachers like Mr. Rock.

Then I applied to twenty-eight colleges and universities. Only two of them were willing to take on the sketchy Winkler kid. I focused on the closest, Emerson College in Boston, a very, very liberal arts school. I chose Emerson in part because I'd heard it was founded as a "school of oratory." I looked up the word *oratory* and saw that it meant "public speaking" or "speechifying."

That sounded so good to me. No more highlighting! Just speechifying!

College wasn't quite that simple, of course. I struggled with many classes, but my theater major helped me survive. Today you will find my name on Emerson's website under Notable Alumni, alongside Jay Leno, Spalding Gray, Denis Leary, and Norman Lear.

Of course, many of my teachers didn't think I was so notable when I was on campus, but I'm glad they think that now. They even gave me an honorary PhD in Hebrew literature a few years ago. Reading Hebrew is a real challenge for a dyslexic, so I'm glad I didn't have to earn that degree the usual way.

I did manage to graduate from Emerson in the allotted time and then, miracle of miracles, I was accepted into the Master of Fine Arts program at the Yale School of Drama! First thing I did was tell my parents. Well, I didn't tell them so much as throw it in their disapproving faces.

I called home and said, "Dumb dog just got into Yale!"

My mother did not exactly jump for joy. She responded wearily with as much enthusiasm as she could muster, in her heavy German accent: "Oh, sis is nice. Tell sis to ir vater."

She quickly handed me off to my father. He was equally underwhelmed.

Very supportive people, my parentals. They were not impressed, either, when I was one of only three applicants accepted into the Yale Repertory Theatre company three years later.

Despite my lack of a home cheering section and my reading and writing challenges, I came to an absurd conclusion at a young age: I simply felt I could accomplish anything I wanted to do.

Not only was I a raging optimist, I was absolutely driven. I had to accomplish everything I wanted in life. So I learned to never give in to fear or negativity. If I never gave up, if I replaced negatives with positives, and if I believed that my dreams could become realities, I was sure I could do anything. Anything!

And I felt I had to do it on my own because my parents just didn't get me. At all. My father, who had an international lumber brokerage and could trade timber in eleven languages, wanted me to sell wood for the rest of my life.

Wood!

They had no respect for my dreams of becoming an actor.

Then, as a young actor, I did thirty commercials. Still not impressed.

A big role in my first movie, *The Lords of Flatbush*, hardly merited a yawn from my folks. And when I landed a recurring role in a network television series, they barely batted an eye.

Only after my *Happy Days* performances won critical and popular acclaim did my parents accept me as their successful son. In fact, they became lobbyists. They would go sit in the lobby of Palm Beach hotels and wave at anyone who passed, telling them in a heavy German accent, "Ve are der Fonzie's parents!"

By that time, I no longer needed their acceptance or approval. I'd learned to make it on my own. Then, in 1973, I had the distinction of opening and closing on Broadway—all in one night. My starring role was in a play called *42 Seconds from Broadway*. Forty-two seconds was actually longer than it lasted.

Still, I did not give up on my dream of performing in a Broadway show. I made a promise to myself on opening-and-closing night, while walking back to my apartment, *I'm going to make it right! I will return to Broadway one day.* I had no idea at the time how I would accomplish this goal, but I'd come to see myself as one of those blow-up cowboys or clowns with sand in the bottom that you knock over, only to have it pop right back up. I might fall down, but I always stand back up, dust myself off, and keep moving forward toward my dreams.

And so, twenty-six years later, Broadway called me back. I think it must have lost my number for a while. The call came from Broadway's most successful playwright, Mr. Neil Simon, who has written more plays than Shakespeare.

"Would you like to read my play aloud with an ensemble so I can hear it performed?" Neil Simon asked.

To an actor, this was like a royal invitation; a chance to perform for the king.

"Send me the script as soon as possible," I said.

Meanwhile, I'm thinking, *I'm dead meat!*

The greatest and most prolific playwright in the history of

Broadway had just asked me to read a part in his play in front of him and his team. I should have been thrilled, right?

By that time, I'd put in ten years on *Happy Days* and three years on *Laverne & Shirley*, not to mention movie roles in *Night Shift*, *Scream*, and *The Waterboy*. I was a well-known actor who'd won some big awards, so I should have been supremely confident.

Nope. It's strange how old insecurities refuse to die. Once again, the "dumb dog" label lifted a hind leg and peed on my self-esteem.

This is the worst thing that has ever happened to me! worried the whiner within.

My fears had some justification. Because of my dyslexia, I have difficulty reading aloud from a script. To compensate, I've learned to memorize most scripts before performing them, even in rehearsals. I was terrified that I would become tangled up and tongue-tied in front of Neil Simon. War raged within my psyche as I came up with excuse after excuse for doing a no-show at the read-through. It was my worst nightmare.

Scared Henry thought, *I don't have to do this. What do I need this for?*

Determined Henry countered, *Are you crazy? This is Neil Simon, you schmuck! This is your passion!*

Finally, it was Daddy Henry who took control of the situation. I didn't want my children to see their father give in to fear. I preach to them day and night that they have to have the courage to make their own dreams reality. I had to walk the talk.

I read for the Bard beater, and what do you know, I didn't embarrass myself. I think he laughed aloud at least once. I felt good about the reading. We shook hands, and I went home. Months later, Broadway called again. Only this time, it was off-off-off Broadway.

"Do you want to do the play downtown at the L.A. Music Center?" asked Mr. Neil Simon's representative.

"Yes, most certainly!" I responded.

I needed to do this show. My career was, shall we say, in a lull. This was a chance to work with some great actors, including my old friends John Ritter, Ed Herrmann, Penny Fuller, and Veanne Cox.

Rehearsals were wonderful. My late friend John Ritter was so funny during rehearsals, breaks, lunches, rides home; it didn't matter where we were, he was razor sharp. We had so much fun.

Then came the dress rehearsal when we actually had to perform for an audience. The venue was the Mark Taper Forum theater, which has an intimate design, placing actors close to the crowd.

I had done mostly television and film acting up to that point. I'd let it slip my mind that in theatrical productions, you act in front of a living, breathing group of people. I felt rusty, and I was scared. Okay, I was petrified. I couldn't make myself walk across the street from our rehearsal hall to the actual theater and the newly constructed set waiting for us.

Stage fright set in at the mere sight of it.

"I'll just real quick hire another actor and teach him my lines and

JOHN AND I STARTED THE PLAY ON STAGE TOGETHER EVERY NIGHT.
JUST THE TWO OF US. I MISS HIM.

movements so he can take over from here," I told the director. "Then I'll just go home and buy a ticket online."

He looked at me as if I was a nine-headed Hydra beast.

So two days later, we rehearsed in front of real people on the new set. I got by with a little help from my friends on stage. Not a single tomato was thrown. Because of the warm response, the producers opened the play for paying audiences. They came. They saw. They weren't nuts about it.

Based on the so-so reviews, the New York producers decided not to produce it in New York. "Thanks, but no thanks," they said.

That was January 2000. The new millennium was not starting out so hot, even though I loved doing the play with John Ritter and I loved the fact that I performed before a live audience without crumpling to the floor and balling up into a fetal position.

Two months later, another call came from Mr. Simon. This time he said the Kennedy Center for the Performing Arts in Washington, D.C., had an opening in its theater schedule. They wanted us to perform *The Dinner Party* in July.

I decided to do it for three big reasons: First of all, the lull in my career was hanging on like a nasty cold. Secondly, the wonderful Broadway star Len Cariou joined the cast. And finally, Neil Simon is not only a brilliant writer, he's a genius rewriter. When *The Dinner Party* was not well received in L.A., he took out his pen and revised the script—eight times. Each time it was Simon-ized, the play improved.

The Dinner Party 9.0 received strong reviews in Washington, D.C. The New York City producers liked it, too. They invited us to bring it to Broadway, for real. We opened on the nineteenth of October, 2000, and we had a very nice run of 364 performances—a year's worth, almost. For nine months, the play was sold out, and we performed for people from all over the country, some of whom had never seen a Broadway play.

Returning to Broadway with a successful show allowed me to realize another major dream, one that I had nurtured since childhood: When I was in high school, we would walk through Central Park at lunchtime, thinking we were really cool ninth graders, and ride the carousel while eating tuna sandwiches. During the spring, I was always late for my after-lunch class because I would stop and watch the Broadway softball league play in the park. Every Broadway show had a team, which included the stars and the crew. I'd long dreamed of one day being a player on a Broadway league team. That dream came true in May 2001, when *The Dinner Party* softball team was formed. For one of the first times in my life, I was a high draft pick. I pitched. My buddy John Ritter was on first. What a team!

I'd made my triumphant return to Broadway and to the Central Park softball diamond. My tenacity and determination paid off. Hey, it took some time, and a couple of tries, but I did it.

And that, finally, brings me back to fly-fishing.

If you have the dream to fly-fish, do it. If you just want to travel to Montana and walk around in wonder at the beauty of the great American West, do it. If you dream of writing a book, taking photographs, skydiving, or touring Italy, make it happen!

Don't give up on your dreams; you can and must make them your reality. We all have insecurities and fears. We all have some disabilities, just as we all have some abilities. You should never allow anything or anybody to define you or keep you from living the best life you can.

Easier said than done, I know. Believe me, I know. I was terrified of performing in *The Dinner Party*, but that fear of doing it was far worse than actually taking the stage. In fact, once I stepped in front of that audience, I had the time of my life. The same holds true for fly-fishing. At first I was scared of failing. Casting seemed to require too much coordination, but I worked and worked at it and eventually I was not so bad anymore. In fact, I was pretty darn good. And I loved it!

Now you know why my fishing vacations are so important to me. This wonderful sport serves as a metaphor for my life. I can fish for an entire day without catching a single trout, and it just doesn't matter . . . much. I can fall down and soak myself in a river and say "So what?" I don't care, I'm just chilly.

Failure may happen to me, but it does not live in me. I taught myself to read, even though I had dyslexia. And I became the coauthor with Lin Oliver of seventeen children's books, which have sold in the millions around the world, and made millions of kids laugh. Imagine that!

THIS PICTURE WAS TAKEN AT THE LAST DRESS REHEARSAL, JUST BEFORE WE OPENED ON BROADWAY IN OCTOBER 2000.

This dumb dog has acted, directed, produced, written, and fly-fished! And he can even be taught new tricks! Over the last two years, Rowan, my patient guide from Firehole Ranch, has taken me to a higher level of fly-fishing skill than I ever dreamed of mastering. I dry cast 90 percent of the time. No fish is safe now.

That's a very good thing for a fly fisherman, but it's an even better thing for Henry Winkler. It's an accomplishment that I can talk about to others who need a Mr. Rock in their lives. I can use each and every one of my accomplishments as a building block that might help boost their self-confidence and self-esteem. I can tell them my story—in my speeches, in my Hank Zipzer books, and in our conversations.

Hopefully, I'm not just talking to them. I'm showing them. I'm giving them a little inspiration—the same helpful stuff that worked for me in my life—to put in their pockets and carry around with them. I take photographs of my fish and my adventures as proof that anything is possible. I keep pushing and moving forward, and if others can see me up ahead, perhaps they will be able to see how rewarding it is, and they will follow at their own pace. They can accompany me on my journey, and I can walk with them on theirs.

I'll be headed back to the river soon. I plan on catching more beautiful trout. If you see me out there, feel free to wish me "tight lines." I wish the same to you. I also wish you the joy that comes from meeting even the smallest challenge head on and realizing it CAN be conquered. And I wish you the serenity that Mother Nature has been so generous in providing me.

I can't wait to see you on the river. Just remember to keep moving along. I'm a good person. I'm just bad at sharing my trout stream.

THE TEAM THAT
MAKES LIFE GLOW: HENRY   JED

ZOE   MAX   STACEY

ACKNOWLEDGMENTS

While sitting at the luncheon table at our oldest son's wedding to his wife, Amanda, I showed a few photographs I had taken over the years while in Montana to Cristina and Tony Thomopolous.

They introduced the idea of a book and then introduced me to Jan Miller.

This book exists because Jan Miller said yes.

We never met.

We never telephoned.

We never e-mailed before this book idea became an idea.

Not only did she say yes, she also found Insight Editions.

And Raoul Goff, Jake Gerli, Jason Babler, Justin Allen, and all the other tasteful folks up there in San Rafael who came into my life.

Along with the pictures, the publisher actually wanted words, too. If you don't know Wes Smith, I suggest you seek him out and try to be his friend. He is an astounding wordsmith who helped me put my river journey into a coherent order.

A gigantic thank-you has to go to Margaret Schrader for all her enthusiastic help in coordinating and calling and retyping and proofreading and all-around support.

Ricardo Perez and Leticia Perez have to be included for keeping us well nourished in body and soul all during the writing process.

My wife, Stacey, and children, Jed, Zoe, and Max, and my daughter-in-law, Amanda, and my son-in-law, Rob, need to be included on this page because of their enormous patience while looking at every picture I've ever taken over and over and over again, always with a smile that never seemed forced. And believe me, I scrutinized.

We cannot forget our first granddaughter, Indya Belle. Yes, she is only sixteen months old, but her cooing and oohing was an absolute factor in our picture selection.

And last but not least, all the guides, all over the world, who kept me untangled.

I acknowledge you all.

I thank you all.

And I am grateful that you are in my life.

THIS IS THE BACK OF OUR CABIN AT THE FIREHOLE RANCH. IT INVITES YOU TO RELAX AND RELIVE THE FISH YOU CAUGHT AND THE ONES THAT GOT AWAY.